The Story of a Special Day
Volume 348

December

13

The 347ᵗʰ day of the year (348ᵗʰ in leap years). There are 18 days remaining until the end of the year.

by Michael Dobson

Timespinner
Press

This book is also available in e-book form for Kindle, e-pub devices, and other formats from your favorite online booksellers.

For more information about the series, about us, or about your special day, please email us at editor@timespinnerpress.com.

Look for other volumes in *The Story of a Special Day,* coming often. See www.timespinnerpress.com for details and for the most recent information.

Table of Contents

For the definition of "O.S.," "N.S.," "CE," and "BCE" used with some dates , see the section "On Names and Dates."

Cover: "Laying the Pontoons at Fredericksburg," by Thure de Thustrup, 1887. The American Civil War Battle of Fredericksburg's bloodiest day of fighting was December 13, 1862 — the **Event of the Day**.

Quote of the Day

"It is well that war is so terrible, otherwise
we should grow too fond of it."

General Robert E. Lee, observing
the battlefield at Fredericksburg,
December 13, 1862

Today
in
History

December 13

Robert E. Lee (Photo: Julian Vannerson)

Ambrose Burnside (Photo: Mathew Brady)

Event of the Day
December 13, 1862 — Battle of Fredericksburg

The American Civil War's Battle of Fredericksburg took place between December 11 and December 15, 1862. General Robert E. Lee's Confederate Army of Northern Virginia defeated the Union Army of the Potomac, commanded by General Ambrose Burnside. The key fighting during that battle took place on December 13.

Prelude to the Battle

The early years of the American Civil War did not go well for the Union. In the Eastern Theatre, the Confederate Army of Northern Virginia defeated Union forces attempting to invade Virginia, and pursued them into the north, where Lee and Union General-in-Chief George McClellan met at at the Battle of Antietam in the bloodiest single day in American history. The Union success gave President Abraham Lincoln the opportunity to issue the Emancipation Proclamation.

At Antietam, Confederate forces were blocked and Lee retreated to Virginia. In spite of repeated demands by the President, McClellan refused to pursue Lee, and as a result, Lincoln removed him from command.

In his place, Lincoln gave the command to General Ambrose Burnside (whose distinctive facial hair became known as "sideburns," derived from his name). Burnside planned a campaign of quick movement and deception, reluctantly approved by Lincoln, but it quickly fell apart when necessary supplies and equipment weren't delivered on time.

Noticing Burnside's slow movement, Lee moved his forces toward Fredericksburg, in the northern part of Virginia, where Burnside would need to cross the Rappahannock River. Although Burnside had only a single pontoon bridge at his disposal, he might yet have succeeded, because only half of Lee's army had arrived by then. Instead, he waited until all the rest of the pontoon bridges were delivered. (The front cover of this book shows the building of pontoons on December 13.)

Meanwhile, Lee's forces were dug in.

December 13, 1862

The crossing of the river took place on December 13, a cold and overcast day.

Burnside had the larger army, over 120,000, compared to Lee's 78,000. Burnside, however, had the more difficult situation, needing to cross the river while under enemy fire. Union forces made multiple frontal assaults against the Confederate lines. They penetrating Stonewall Jackson's first defensive line once, but were repulsed. Several other assaults failed, with heavy losses each time.

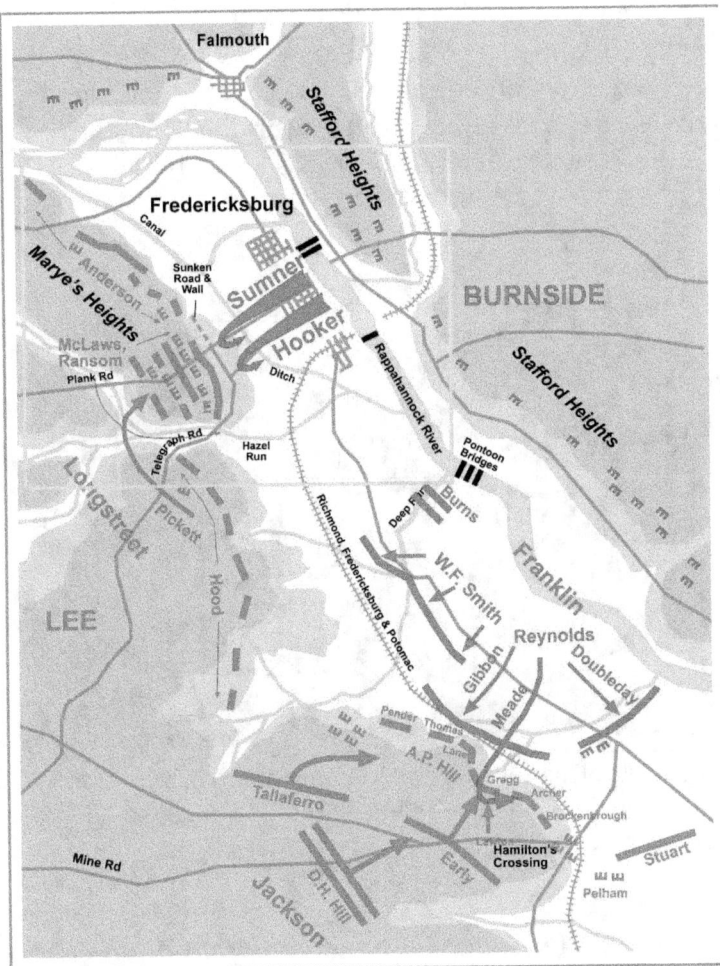

Map of the Battle of Fredericksburg, by Hal Jespersen

At the end of that day, Burnside ordered one final attack for December 14, but his generals persuaded him otherwise. Instead, he asked Lee for a truce to retrieve wounded, and on December 15, retreated back across the river. Union losses were over 12,000, compared to Confederate casualties of 4,200. One witness described the battle to Abraham Lincoln, saying "It was not a battle, it was a butchery."

Aftermath of the battle, showing the destruction of a Confederate caisson by cannon fire.

Aftermath

The Confederate victory at Fredericksburg caused jubilation throughout the South. In the North, Lincoln was widely condemned as a "weak man," and his administration was considered to be in political jeopardy.

Lincoln relieved Burnside of command, replacing him with General Joseph Hooker, but Hooker did no better. He was defeated at the Battle of Chancellorsville in May of the following year, and replaced by General George Meade.

Meade was in command of Union forces at the Battle of Gettysburg in July 1863, the bloodiest battle of the war and generally considered its turning point. Lee's defeat at Gettysburg ended any serious chance of a Confederate victory. Meade, however, failed to intercept Lee's retreat, causing Lincoln to turn to a new leader from the Western Theater of the war, Ulysses S. Grant.

Today

The Civil War Trust is funding battlefield preservation at the historic Slaughter Pen Farm, the largest remaining unprotected part of the battlefield, and the only place a visitor can follow the December 13 Union assault from beginning to end.

The 2003 film *Gods and Generals* (based on the novel of the same name by Jeffrey Shaara) chronicles the Battle of Fredericksburg. Louisa May Alcott, famous for Little Women, nursed soldiers after the battle, fictionalized in her 1863 book *Hospital Sketches.*

Sir Francis Drake, by Henry Bone (1829)

What Happened on December 13?

From the creation of great works of engineering and art, to devastating wars and natural disasters, thousands of years of history have left their mark on each and every day of the year. Here are some important events that occurred on December 13. (Items with a photo or illustration are boxed.)

1577 — **Sir Francis Drake** departs England with a fleet of five ships to sail around the world. The circumnavigation will take three years.

1769 — **Dartmouth College**, one of the nine colonial colleges chartered before the American Revolution, is founded in New Hampshire.

1928 — George Gershwin's *An American in Paris* premiers at Carnegie Hall.

1937 — The **Battle of Nanjing** ends after thirteen days with a Japanese victory, and the **Nanjing Massacre** (also called the Rape of Nanjing) begins. The massacre will last six weeks, with a death toll estimated as high as 300,000.

1939 — The first naval battle of the Second World War, the **Battle of the River Plate** (near Argentina and Uruguay) takes place between the German cruiser *Admiral Graf Spee* and a hunting group of three British Royal Navy ships. Damage to the *Graf Spee* results in that ship being scuttled four days later.

1968 — The military dictatorship in Brazil issues Ato Institucional Número Cinco (**AI-5**), which suspends all constitutional protections and institutionalizes the use of torture. It will be repealed by constitutional amendment ten years later.

1972 — The last of three moonwalks during the **Apollo 17** mission takes place. It is, at the time of writing, the last occasion when humans walked on the surface of the Moon.

1977 — An Air Indiana DC-3 flight carrying the **University of Evansville (Indiana) basketball team** crashes shortly after takeoff, killing all but one team member, who had missed the flight. That person was killed by drunk driver two weeks later.

2003 — Former Iraqi president **Saddam Hussein is captured** by US forces while hiding in a hole.

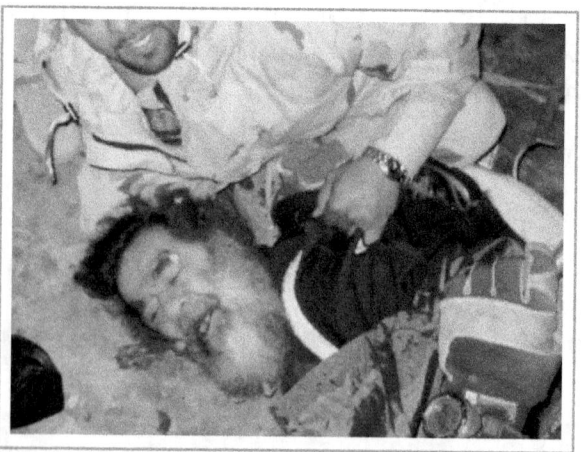

Capture of Saddam Hussein

Apollo 17 astronaut Eugene Cernan on the last moonwalk,
December 13, 1972 (Photo: Harrison Schmitt)

Quote of the Day

"Ordinarily he is insane, but he has lucid moments when he is only stupid."

Heinrich Heine, essayist and poet
born December 13, 1797

Births and Deaths

December 13

Sgt. Alvin C. York, World War I Medal of Honor winner
He was played by Gary Cooper in the 1941 film *Sergeant York*.
York was born on December 13, 1887.

Notable December 13 People

With the current world population at about seven billion people, on average about 19 million people also celebrate their birthdays on December 13 — and that isn't counting millions and millions who came before! No matter when you were born, you share your birthday with many special people whose accomplishments (and occasionally embarrassments) have been noted as part of history.

In this section, you'll meet fascinating people who share your birthday. They're organized by what they're famous for, and then in reverse chronological order from most recent to earliest. Those who are shown in photographs or artwork have a box around them. We don't have photos of everyone, so please forgive us if your favorite person is missing.

Some of these people you've heard of, others will be new to you, but they all make up an important part of the reason that December 13 is a truly special day!

Dick Van Dyke (center) from The Dick Van Dyke Show, with Mary Tyler Moore on the left and Larry Mathews on the right. Dick Van Dyke was born December 13, 1925

Who Was Born on December 13?

Art

Emily Carr, artist and writer described as a "Canadian icon." *(1945)*

"Breton Church," Emily Carr (1906)

Business and Technology

Ben Bernanke, US economist who served as Chairman of the Federal Reserve during the financial crisis of the late 2000s. *(1953)*

Werner von Siemens, German inventor who founded the Siemens Corporation; the unit of electrical conductance is named the *siemens* in his honor. *(1816)*

Johann Wolfgang Döbereiner, chemist who invented the Döbereiner lamp (tinderbox), the first lighter. Over a million were sold to light fires and pipes. *(1780)*

Government and Politics

Herman Cain, American business executive and politician known for his unsuccessful campaign to become the 2012 Republican nominee for US President. *(1945)*

Prince Aga Khan IV, hereditary *imam* (spiritual leader) of the Nizari Isma'ilist denomination of Islam; one of the ten richest royals with an estimated net worth of US$800 million. *(1936)*

Ella Baker, African-American civil rights activist who worked with or mentored many of the most famous civil rights leaders of her day; called "perhaps the most influential woman in the Civil Rights Movement." *(1903)*

Mary Todd Lincoln, First Lady during the administration of her husband, Abraham Lincoln. *(1818)*

Mary Todd Lincoln (Brady-Handy Collection)

Journalism and Literature

Drew Pearson, well-known journalist who wrote the syndicated newspaper column "Washington Merry-Go-Round." *Time* Magazine said his column sent four Congressmen to jail and caused the resignation of Eisenhower's chief of staff. *(1897)*

Heinrich Heine, German poet, journalist, and critic. His works have been set to music by such composers as Schumann, Schubert, Mendelssohn, Brahms, Tchaikovsky, and Wagner. *(1797)*

Military

Sergeant Alvin C. York, received the Medal of Honor during World War I for leading an attack on a German machine gun nest, taking 35 guns; killing at least 28 Germans, and capturing 132 more. His story was dramatised in the 1941 film *Sergeant York,* with Gary Cooper receiving a Best Actor Oscar for his starring role. *(1887) (Photo page 12.)*

Music

Taylor Swift, singer-songwriter who has won ten Grammys, an Emmy, and five Guinness World Records. Named as one of the 100 most influential people in the world by *Time* Magazine. *(1989)*

Tom DeLonge, co-founder, guitarist, and co-lead vocalist of Blink-182. *(1975)*

John Anderson, country musician who charted more than 40 singles on the *Billboard* country music charts. *(1954)*

Berton Averre, lead guitarist for The Knack, known for their #1 hit song "My Sharona." *(1953)*

Randy Owen, country music performer known as the lead singer of the country rock band Alabama. *(1949)*

Ted Nugent, lead guitarist for the Amboy Dukes and later a successful solo artist; known for strongly expressed conservative political views.

Jeff "Skunk" Baxter, guitarist for Steely Dan and the Doobie Brothers; later a consultant in missile defense technology. *(1948)*

Carlos Montoya, flamenco guitarist credited with transforming flamenco guitar music into its own style. *(1903)*

Performing Arts

Jamie Foxx, won a Best Actor Oscar for playing Ray Charles in the 2004 film *Ray;* also known for *Collateral, Jarhead,*and *Django Unchained,* as well as the TV series *The Jamie Foxx Show* and *In Living Color.*

Steve Buscemi, actor known for roles in the TV series *The Sopranos* and *Boardwalk Empire;* as well as such films as *Reservoir Dogs, Con Air,* and *The Big Lebowski.* *(1957)*

Wendie Malick, actress known for roles on such sitcoms as *Dream On, Just Shoot Me!,* and *Hot in Cleveland. (1950)*

John Davidson, actor and game show host known for such shows as *That's Incredible!, Hollywood Squares,* and *The $100,000 Pyramid.* (1941)

Richard D. Zanuck, film producer and son of Darryl F. Zanuck; won the Academy Award for Best Picture for 1989's *Driving Miss Daisy* and helped launch the careers of Steven Spielberg and Tim Burton. *(1934)*

Christopher Plummer, actor known for roles in *The Sound of Music, The Return of the Pink Panther, The Man Who Would Be King,* and *The Thorn Birds.* Oldest actor to ever win an Academy Award. *(1929)*

Dick Van Dyke, known for the 1960s sitcom *The Dick Van Dyke Show,* and for such films as *Bye Bye Birdie, Mary Poppins,* and *Chitty Chitty Bang Bang;* received a Life Achievement Award from the Screen Actors Guild. *(1925) (Photo page 14.)*

Van Heflin, character actor who won an Academy Award for his performance in the 1942 film *Johnny Eager. (1908)*

Edward LeSaint, Hollywood actor and director during the silent film era; acted in more than 300 films and directed more than 90. *(1870)*

Christopher Plummer, with Julie Andrews in *The Sound of Music*

Science and Mathematics

Philip Warren Anderson, American physicist who won the 1977 Nobel Prize in Physics.

Trygve Haavelmo, Norwegian economist who won the 1989 Nobel Memorial Prize in Economic Sciences for his work in the field of econometrics. *(1911)*

George Pólya, Hungarian-American mathematician; three prizes in mathematics are named for him. *(1867)*

Kristian Birkeland, Norwegian scientist who first determined the nature of the aurora borealis. *(1867)*

Sports

Rickie Fowler, top-ranked amateur golfer in the world for 37 weeks in 2007 and 2008; career high fourth in official world golf rankings. *(1988)*

Chris Grant, Australian rules footballer; member of the Australian Football Hall of Fame. *(1972)*

Sergei Fedorov, Russian ice hockey player with teh Detroit Red Wings and other teams; member of the Ice Hockey Hall of Fame and the International Ice Hockey Federation Hall of Fame. *(1969)*

Rex and Rob Ryan, fraternal twin American football players and coaches for numerous teams. *(1962)*

Gary Zimmerman, offensive lineman for the Minnesota Vikings and Denver Broncos. *(1961)*

Richard Dent, football defensive end primarily for the Chicago Bears; elected to the Pro Football Hall of Fame. *(1960)*

Bob Gainey, hockey player, coach, and executive; inducted into the Hockey Hall of Fame. *(1953)*

Ferguson Jenkins, baseball pitcher who became the first Canadian inducted into the National Baseball Hall of Fame. *(1942)*

Kenneth Hall, American football player nicknamed "Sugar Land Express;" established 17 national football records while still in high school; later played at college and professional levels. *(1935)*

George Rhoden, Jamaican runner who won two Olympic gold medals in the 1952 Helsinki games.

Larry Doby, Negro League baseball player who became the second black player to break the color barrier in that sport; member of the National Baseball Hall of Fame. *(1923)*

Bowman Gum 1951 baseball card of Larry Doby

Bill Vukovich, American racing driver named to the International Motorsports Hall of Fame and the Motorsports Hall of Fame in America; won two Indianapolis 500 races as well as two national championships. *(1918)*

Archie Moore, boxer who held the World Light Heavyweight Championship title for ten years, the longest reign of all time. *(1916)*

"Delicate Tension," Wassily Kandinsky (1923)

Who Died on December 13?

Adventure

Alexander Selkirk, Royal Navy officer who spent four years as a castaway on a Pacific island, whose story helped inspire Daniel Defoe's *Robinson Crusoe.* *(1721)*

Art

Grandma Moses, highly respected American folk artist who who did not begin painting seriously until the age of 78. She lived to be 101 years old. *(1961)*

Wassily Kandinsky (Василий Кандинский), Russian painter and art theorist, known for painting one of the first recognized purely abstract works of art. *(1944)*

Donatello, Florentine Renaissance sculptor considered one of the most important figures in 15th century Italian art. *(1466)*

Crime and Punishment

Stanley Williams, gang member known as a founder and leader of the West Side Crips street gang in Los Angeles; executed after being convicted of the murder of four people. *(2005)*

Josef Kramer, Nazi concentration camp commandant known as the Beast of Belsen; hanged for war crimes. *(1945)*

Irma Grese, Nazi concentration camp guard known as the "Hyena of Auschwitz," youngest woman hanged for war crimes. *(1945)*

Government and Economics

Thomas Schelling, shared the 2005 Nobel Memorial Prize in Economic Sciences for his work in understanding conflict and cooperation using game-theory analysis. *(2016)*

William Roth, Jr., US senator and representative known for sponsoring the legislation that created the Roth IRA retirement savings vehicle. *(2003)*

Samuel Gompers, leader in the American labor movement; founded the American Federation of Labor (AFL) and served as its first president. *(1466)*

Journalism and Literature

Russell Hoban, fantasy, science fiction, and mainstream writer whose best known work is the 1980 novel *Riddley Walker. (2011)*

Samuel Johnson, English writer and editor whose 1755 work *A Dictionary of the English Language* became the pre-eminent British dictionary; subject of the famous biography *The Life of Samuel Johnson,* by James Boswell. *(1784)*

Samuel Johnson, by Joshua Reynolds (1775)

Lupe Vélez

Military

Raymond A. Spruance, admiral who commanded US naval forces in two of the most significant Pacific naval battles in World War II, the Battle of Midway and the Battle of the Philippine Sea, nicknamed the "electric brain" for his calmness during crisis situations. *(1969)*

Music

Zal Yanovsky, lead guitarist and co-founder of the Lovin' Spoonful. *(2002)*

Chuck Schuldiner, singer-songwriter and guitarist known as the "godfather of death metal.". *(2001)*

Performing Arts

Alan Thicke, actor and host known for the sitcom *Growing Pains* and the talk show *Thicke of the Night.* *(2016)*

Floyd "Red Crow" Westerman, Sioux musician, activist, and actor; known for such films as *Dances With Wolves, The Doors,* and *Renegades. (2007)*

Smita Patil, award-winning Indian actress who appeared in more than 80 films. *(1986)*

Lupe Vélez, Mexican actress and comedienne known for her "Mexican Spitfire" films, from which she got her nickname. *(1944)*

Science and Medicine

António Egas Moniz, Portuguese neurologist who shared the 1949 Nobel Prize in Physiology or Medicine for the development of cerebral angiography. *(1955)*

Victor Grignard, French chemist who won the 1912 Nobel Prize in Chemistry for discovering the Grignard reaction. *(1935)*

Fritz Pregl, Slovene-German chemist who won the 1923 Nobel Prize in Chemistry for his contributions to quantitative organic microanalysis. *(1930)*

Niccolò Fontana Tartaglia, Italian mathematician and engineer who was the first to apply mathematics in investigating the path of cannonballs, the foundation of ballistics. *(1557)*

Al-Bīrūnī (البيروني), Iranian scholar and polymath during the Islamic Golden Age; made contributions to numerous fields of science and history. *(1048)*

Sports

Vivian Kellogg, played first base in the All-American Girls Professional Baseball League from 1944 to 1950. *(2013)*

Lamar Hunt, sports entrepreneur who founded a number of different teams; member of the Pro Football Hall of Fame, the National Soccer Hall of Fame, and the International Tennis Hall of Fame. *(2006)*

December, Joachim von Sandrart (1642)

Quote of the Day

"If our animosities are born out of fear, then confident generosity is born out of hope."

Aga Khan IV, spiritual leader,
born December 13, 1936

Holidays
Around
the World

December 13

A large advent calendar in Germany. The **Advent Season** consists
of the four weeks prior to Christmas, which always includes
December 13. (Photo: Kora27, CC BY-SA 4.0)

Holidays Around the World

If you're looking for a reason to take your special day off, you should know that every single day is a holiday somewhere in the world! Here's some of what you can celebrate on December 13!

General Events

Acadian Remembrance Day (Acadian community)

Acadia was a French colony that included much of modern Quebec, the Maritime provinces, and northern Maine. It was later conquered by the British. Today, the term Acadia refers to those areas where Acadians, people with French roots, French language, or French culture are prominent. Acadians became known as Cajuns when they settled Louisiana. Acadian Remembrance Day, held each December 13, commemorates their history and culture.

Dzień Pamięci Ofiar Stanu Wojennego (Poland)

Victims of martial law in Poland are honored on Martial Law Victims Remembrance Day, the anniversary of the declaration of martial law in Poland, December 13, 1981.

Hari Nusantara (Indonesia)
The boundaries of the Indonesian archipelago were formally recognized beginning on December 13, 1957.

Jum ir-Repubblika (Malta)
On December 13, 1974, Malta became an independent republic within the British commonwealth, celebrated as Republic Day.

Nanking Massacre Memorial Day (China)
China honors the thousands of lives lost during the Nanking Massacre*, which began December 13, 1938.

National Day (Saint Lucia)
The Caribbean island nation of Saint Lucia, named for Saint Lucy, has its national day on Saint Lucy's Day†.

Dia do Marinheiro (Brazil)
Many nations honor their military services on special days. Sailor's Day in Brazil is celebrated on December 13.

---

* See page 7.

† See page 40.

Food Days

In the United States, almost every day of the year is dedicated to a particular food. (Some other countries also have official food days, but only in America is there one every single day!) Sponsored by manufacturers, retailers, farmers, or simply fans, these days are often proclaimed by the President, Congress, state governors, or mayors. Given that there are more different foods than days of the year, some days honor more than one kind of food!

In the US, December 13 is **National Hot Cocoa Day** as well as **National Ambrosia Day.**

"A Cup of Hot Chocolate," Pierre-Auguste Renoir
for **National Hot Cocoa Day**

Cocoa beverages have been around a lot longer than you'd think, dating back over 2000 years to Aztec culture. It made its way to Europe from Mexico, where it was used as a medicine to treat liver and stomach diseases well into the 19th century! The current (2012) record holder for the fastest time to drink a hot chocolate is Freddie Flintoff, who did it in 5.45 seconds. Personally, we prefer to sip ours.

In Greek mythology, **ambrosia** is the food of the gods, conferring immortality on all who eat it. Our modern ambrosia is a little less ambitious, a fruit salad that usually includes pineapple, mandarin oranges, marshmallows, and whipped cream, though there are many variations. Its connection to the Greek gods is unknown; it's thought to be an American invention from the late 19th century, presumably after hot cocoa ceased to be medicinal.

Food Months

In addition, the entire month of December is used to celebrate numerous foods.With Christmas on the horizon, it shouldn't be surprising that December is ! **National Egg Nog Month, National Fruit Cake Month,** and **National Pear Month**.

December is also **Food Service Safety Month**. That's probably why the first week in December is **National Handwashing Week**.

Religious Feast Days and Holidays

Hanukkah (חֲנֻכָּה) (Judaism)

The Jewish celebration of Hanukkah, also known as the Festival of Lights or the Feast of Dedication, takes place for eight days and nights beginning on the 25th day of Kislev, which varies from late November to late December. It commemorates the rededication of the Second Temple in Jerusalem at the time of the Maccabean Revolt.

Each night of Hanukkah is marked by lighting one branch of the Menorah, a candelabrum with nine branches. In addition to prayers, celebrants eat foods fried or baked in olive oil. Children play with a spinning top known as a *dreidel* and receive *Hanukkah gelt*.

18th century painting of a Hanukkah celebration, artist unknown.

Saint Lucy's Day (Christianity)

Saint Lucy was a Christian martyr who died in the early 300s during the last major persecution of Christians in the Roman Empire. Her feast day is December 13.

Because her celebration falls near the Winter Solstice (December 21-23 depending on the year), it has become a festival of light. In Scandinavia in particular, it is an occasion for feasts and celebration, filled with light. Saint Lucy's Day is also celebrated in parts of Italy, Hungary, and Croatia.

Saint Days

Each day in the year is considered a feast day for one or more saints. They are somewhat different in western Christianity (Catholicism and many forms of Protestantism) and in eastern (Orthodox) Christianity.

In *Western Christianity*, December 13 is the feast day of Saints, Autbert, Einhildis and Roswinda, Elizabeth Rose, and Jodoc.

In *Eastern Orthodox Christianity*, it is also the commemoration of Saints Ezra, Judith, Miriam, Sarah, Susanna, Columba of Terryglass, Odilia of Asacem, Edburga of Minster-in-Thanet, Tassio Wilfrid, Mardarius, Dositheus, and Neophytos. (These saints are honored on November 30 by "Old Calendrists ‡.")

---

‡ "Old Calendrists" use the Julian calendar rather than the modern Gregorian calendar. December 13 on the Gregorian calendar is November 30 on the Julian. See "What Day of the Week is December 13?"

Saint Lucy, by Benvenuto Tisi

Karthikai Deepam (கார்த்திகை விளக்கீடு) (Hindu Tamil)

The Hindu Tamil celebration of Karthikai Deepam takes place in mid-November to mid-December when the moon is in conjunction with the Pleiades (*Karthigai*). It is a religious festival of lamps and also celebrates the bonding between brothers and sisters.

Honorary Months

Presidents, Congresses, and nations around the world issue proclamations recognizing particular months to honor certain causes. These events generally fall in December, though honorary months do come and go. If not otherwise specified, all months are US. Here are some honorary designations for December.

- Bingo's Birthday Month (the game, not the dog)
- National Critical Infrastructure Protection Month
- National Impaired Driving Prevention Month
- National Sign Up for Summer Camp Month
- National Stress-Free Family Holiday Month
- Safe Toys and Gifts Month
- Spiritual Literacy Month
- Universal Human Rights Month
- Write a Business Plan Month

Bingo card (Photo: Abbey Hendrickson, CC BY-SA 2.0) — for
Bingo's Birthday Month

Moveable and Multi-Day Events

Some events take place over a specific week or time period. Start and finish dates may vary from year to year. Some events occur on different days each year (such as "fourth Saturday of a month"). These events sometimes take place on December 13.

Third Sunday Before Christmas

- Detinjci (Детињци), when children give presents in Serbia

Second Monday Before Christmas

- Green Monday (best sales day for eBay)
- National Tree Planting Day (Malawi)

Friday the Thirteenth

While December 13 doesn't come on Friday every year (see "What Day of the Week is December 13"), sooner or later, every 13th day of the month eventually lands on the last day of the work week.

Friday the 13th is considered an unlucky day in many (but not all) Western nations. Both the number 13 and Friday have a history of being thought unlucky, so when you put the two together, some people begin to worry. The idea that Friday is unlucky seems to be a maritime superstition — sailors believed it was unlucky to start a voyage on a Friday.

As far as the number 13 goes, there are a number of theories.One theory is that it refers to the 13 people around the table at the Last Supper, one of whom (Judas) would shortly betray Jesus. Others point out that on Friday, October 13, 1307, the Knights Templar were arrested, and many of them were later tortured and killed.

Fear of the number thirteen is common enough that a psychological condition, *triskaidekaphobia*, is named for it! (Fear of Friday the 13th in particular is known as *paraskevidekatriaphobia*.) According to some researchers, between 17 and 21 million people in the US alone are bothered by Friday the 13th. Fear of thirteen is so common that many tall buildings skip 13 when numbering floors.

In Spanish-speaking countries, as well as in Greece, they worry about Tuesday the 13th (*martes trece*) instead —though either way, December 13 qualifies. In Italy, though, 13 is a lucky number — but watch out for Friday the 17th!

Friday the Thirteenth (Photo: W. J. Pilsak, CC BY-SA 3.0)

Quote of the Day

"Ooh, with a little luck —
December will be magic again."

Kate Bush, singer-songwriter
"December Will be Magic Again"

About
the
Month
of

December

"December," from the *Brevarium Grimani* by Simon Bening (c.1510)

December: The Twelfth Month

"In cold December fragrant chaplets blow,
And heavy harvests nod beneath the snow."

— Alexander Pope, *Dunciad*.

In Latin, *decem* means "ten," so it may seem strange that December is actually the twelfth month of the year. The original Roman calendar, from which our month names come, began in March, making December indeed the tenth month.

No one is completely sure when the start of the year was moved to January, but the traditional name of December stuck.

In the northern hemisphere, December is the month with the shortest daylight hours of the year; in the southern hemisphere, it's the opposite. December is the equivalent of June in the southern hemisphere, and vice versa.

In the Julian and Gregorian calendars, December is the twelfth and last month of the year, and is one of seven months with 31 days.

In every year, December starts on the same day of the week as September, and ends on the same day of the week as April.

The length of the day varies through the year, because the Earth tilts as it revolves around the Sun. The two extremes are known as the *solstices*, and the points at which day and night are of equal length are known as the *equinoxes*. The northern hemisphere's winter solstice, which is the shortest day of the year, falls in December. In the southern hemisphere, the summer solstice, the longest day of the year, falls in December.

The dates of the solstice can vary between December 20 and 22. Because even the ancients could tell when the days stopped getting shorter (or longer) and started in the other direction, many holidays and festivals take place around the time of the solstice, including most famously Christmas.

"December," by Gabriel Perelle

December in Other Cultures

In Albanian, the month of December is known as *Dhjetor*. In Egyptian Arabic, it's ديسمبر (pronounced *dīsambar*). In Czech, it's *Prosinec,* in Finland it's *Joulukuu,* and in Poland it's *Grudzień.* Hungarians say *Karácsony hava.*

In Greek, the month of Δεκέμβριος is pronounced *Dekémbrios*. In Hebrew, it's דצמבר and Hindi, it's दिसंबर.

In Irish Gaelic, the month of December is *Nollaig mi na Nollag* and in Scottish Gaelic it's *an Dùbhlachd.* The Welsh say *Rhagfyr.*

The Chinese and Japanese both write the month 十二月, but it is pronounced differently in Cantonese, Mandarin, and Japanese. Koreans write it as 십이월, or *Sipiweol*. In Vietnam it's 腩进仁 *(Tháng mười hai)*.

In Old English, the month is *Gēolmōnaþ* and in Anglo-Saxon it's *Ærra-ġēola mōnaþ.*

The month of December does not correspond exactly with months in other calendar systems. The Hebrew months of כִּסְלֵו (*Kislev*) and טֵבֵת (*Tevet*) overlap December, as do the Persian months of آذر (*Azar*) and دی (*Dey*) and the Hindu months of मार्गशीर्ष (*Mārgaśirṣa*) and पूस (*Pauṣa*).

In the Islamic world, the lunar calendar consists of 354 or 355 days, meaning that the months slowly migrate through the year, and over time different months correspond to December.

December Sayings and Superstitions

- "A green December fills the graveyard."
- "When December snows fall fast, marry and true love will last."
- "A December bride will be fond of novelty, entertaining but extravagant."
- "Married in days of December's cheer / Love's star shines brighter from year to year."

Which day should you marry? That's easy.

> "Monday for health
> Tuesday for wealth
> Wednesday best of all
> Thursday for losses
> Friday for crosses
> Saturday for no luck at all."

According to legend, auspicious dates for December weddings are 1, 8, 10, 19, 23, and 29.

December Symbols

Birthstone: December birthstones in various traditions include turquoise, lapiz lazuli, zircon, blue topaz, and tanzanite.

Oil painting on lapis lazuli, *Perseus Rescuing Andromeda*, by Giuseppe Cesari.

Michael Dobson

Birth Flowers: December's flowers are the narcissus and the holly.

Illustration by Anton Hartinger from *Atlas der Alpenflora* (1882)

"December," by Eugène Grasset

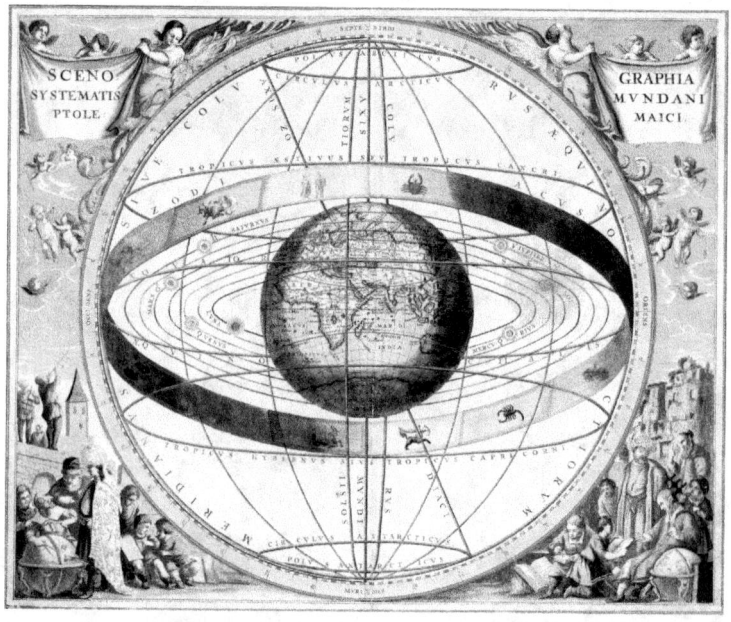

Scenography of the Ptolemaic Cosmography, by Johannes van Loon, based on Andreas Cellarius's *Harmonia Macrocosmica,* 1660

December 13 Zodiac Signs

From the perspective of someone on Earth, the Sun appears to move through the sky throughout the year, along a path astronomers call the *ecliptic plane*. The ecliptic plane is divided into twelve constellations, known as the zodiac, based on traditionally observed patterns of stars. On your birthday, you can't see your constellation, because it's in the daytime sky.

The zodiac was first developed by Babylonian astronomers about 2,500 years ago. Because they were unaware that the Earth wobbles like a spinning top (known as *precession*), they didn't make allowance for the fact that the Sun's path through the zodiac changes over time.

That means there are now two sets of dates for your birth sign. The *tropical dates* are the original Babylonian dates; the *sidereal dates* tell you where the Sun actually appears as it moves along its annual path.

For December 13, the tropical sign is **Sagittarius** and the sidereal sign is **Scorpio**.

Sagittarius

Tropical November 23 to December 21
Sidereal December 16 to January 14

Sagittarius means "archer" in Latin. The constellation in the night sky is often depicted as having the appearance of a stick-figure archer drawing its bow.

The brighter stars in Sagittarius form an asterism known as The Teapot. The Milky Way is densest in Sagittarius, because the galactic center lies in that direction.

In astrology, Sagittarius is a fire sign. People born under it are said to be not superstitious. They are supposed to be drawn toward travel and philosophy, and to enjoy social contacts, meeting new people, and exploring other cultures. They are also said to be highly intelligent, visionary, and tolerant.

Sagittarians are considered compatible with Aries, Leo, and Gemini, and to a lesser extent with Taurus and Virgo.

Scorpio

Tropical October 23 to November 21
Sidereal November 16 to December 15

Scorpio, the Scorpion, appears in the Greek myth of the hunter Orion. Because Orion had touched the robes of the goddess Artemis, in revenge, the goddess had the scorpion kill Orion. As a reward, she placed the scorpion in the sky, where it chases Orion through the eternal night.

The constellation of Scorpius includes the red giant star Antares, which is so large that the entire Solar System through the orbit of Mars would be inside it.

Scorpio is a fire sign, and people born under this sign are supposed to be determined, reserved, loyal, and secretive. Scorpios are supposed to be compatible with the water signs of Pisces and Capricorn.

Illustration by Edward Penfield

What Day of the Week is December 13?

On what day of the week does December 13 fall?

Surprisingly, this isn't an easy question. Because the calendar year is 365 days long (366 in leap years), it doesn't divide evenly by the seven days of the week.

Also, the Earth goes around the Sun in about 365-1/4 days, so a calendar tends to drift over time. That's why the same date falls on different weekdays in different years.

This is made even more complicated by a change in calendars that took place in 1582. Our modern calendar has its roots in ancient Rome, in a calendar reform conducted by Julius Caesar. Caesar commissioned mathematicians to attack the problem, and they came up with the idea of leap years, and thus standardized the calendar for centuries to come. This was called the Julian calendar.

Over time, however, the small errors in Caesar's calculation compounded. That's why Pope Gregory XIII commissioned the Gregorian calendar, used in most of the world today. Some countries converted in 1582, when the calendar was first developed; some converted later; other still haven't changed.

Gregorian and Julian aren't the only types of calendars. The Hebrew year, the Islamic year, and many other calendars are used in different parts of the world and among different people.

You can convert Gregorian dates to other calendars, including the Hebrew calendar, the Islamic calendar, and even the Mayan calendar by visiting the Fourmilab Calendar Converter at http://www.fourmilab.ch/documents/calendar/.

Chinese calendar systems are quite complex and have changed several times; a full discussion is far beyond the scope of this book. If you're interested, you can find information here: http://www.hermetic.ch/cal_stud/chinese_cal.htm.

On Names and Dates

Historians use "CE" (Common Era) and "BCE" (Before the Common Era) instead of the more common "AD" (Anno Domini, or Year of Our Lord) and "BC" (Before Christ), reflecting the fact that the year-numbering system established by the Gregorian calendar is used throughout the world in many countries not culturally Christian.

The CE/BCE designation dates back to at least 1708, and has been adopted as a standard by the United Nations and the Universal Postal Union. Because this series of books covers events and people of all nations and cultures, we use the CE/BCE terms.

The abbreviation "O.S." ("Old Style") and "N.S." ("New Style") on some dates refers to the fact that the Russian Empire (in particular) did not switch from the Julian to the Gregorian calendar at the same time as the rest of Europe, and therefore some figures and events have two dates.

Also, in the Julian calendar in England in the 16th century, the year began on March 25 rather than January 1. To avoid confusion with Gregorian dates, dates between January and March were often written using both years.

People and events whose original names are not in the Western alphabet have their native names (where possible) in the appropriate script shown in parenthesis. If you are using an e-reader to access an electronic version of this book, all characters don't always display on all devices.

A 50-year brass perpetual calendar.

Quote of the Day

"Time is an illusion, lunchtime doubly so."

Douglas Adams,
from *The Hitchhiker's Guide to the Galaxy*

Notes
and
Credits

Timespinner
Press

Cartoon by John T. McCutcheon

Copyright, Credit, and Contact

Follow Us

Our blog "This Day in History" (http://
timespinnerpress.com/this-day-in-history/) features short
articles on events and people associated with each day, and
updates several times each week. Also subscribe to the
"Quote of the Day" at http://timespinnerpress.com/quote-
of-the-day/. You can get daily links by following us on
Facebook at TimespinnerPress, or on Twitter as
@sidewisethinker.

Contact Us

Find an error or a format problem? Want information about
the series, about us, or about when the volume for your
special day might be available? Please email us at
editor@timespinnerpress.com. (We also take requests if your
special day isn't yet complete. Please give us at least six
weeks' notice if possible.)

Sources

We owe a great debt to Wikipedia, which is our first stop for
research. We attempt to make independent confirmation of
all important dates and facts through a variety of other
sources.

Other sources we frequently use include the Library of
Congress; "on this day" listings from *Encyclopedia Britannica*,
the *New York Times*, and the BBC; Omniglot for the names of
months in other languages; *Chase's Calendar of Events*; and, of
course, the always essential Google.

All art and photographs are either in the public domain, used under a Creative Commons license, or with a "fair use" justification, and most frequently come from Wikimedia Commons and the Library of Congress Prints and Photographs Division.

Attribution is provided where possible, or as requested by the copyright owner, or when there is particular historical significance, listed below. For information about any particular illustration or photograph, please contact us.

Credits

1. The illustration "Laying the Pontoons at Fredericksburg" by Thure de Thustrup was published May 16, 1887, and is in the public domain because its copyright has expired. The image is from the collections of the Library of Congress, digital ID cph.3b53081. The image has been cropped because of the dimensions of the cover.

2. The illustration of the month of December used on the back cover is from the French Gothic illuminated manuscript *Les Très Riches Heures du duc de Berry* by the Limbourg Brothers, Jean Colombe, and an intermediate painter whose name is lost to history. It is in the public domain because its copyright has expired.

3. The box graphic used on the first page is from a 1916 pamphlet entitled "Divorce versus Democracy" authored by G. K. Chesterton, originally published in London by the Society of St. Peter and St. Paul. It is in the public domain in the US because it was published prior to 1923, and is in the public domain in all countries (including the country of origin) in which the copyright time is the author's life plus 70 years or less.

4. The graphic design for the section pages in this book is from a design originally created for a pharmacy label. It is courtesy of Wellcome Images (ICV No 11073, photo V0010813), and is used here under CC BY-SA 4.0.

5. The 1864 photograph of General Robert E. Lee was taken by Julian Vannerson, and is in the public domain because its

copyright has expired. It is from the Library of Congress, digital ID cwpb.04402.

6. The photograph of General Ambrose Burnside was taken by Mathew Brady sometime between 1860 and 1865, and is in the public domain because its copyright has expired. It is from the Library of Congress Civil War Photographs Collection, reproduction number LC-DIG-cwpb-05368.

7. The 2006 map of the Battle of Fredericksburg was drawn by Hal Jespersen, who released it into the public domain.

8. The photograph "Havoc" (aftermath of the Battle of Fredericksburg) is from the Defense Visual Information Center, ID: HD-SN-99-01916.

9. The US Army photograph of the 2003 capture of Saddam Hussein is in the public domain as a work created by a soldier or employee of the US government as part of that person's official duties. The image has been cropped.

10. The picture of Apollo 17 astronaut Eugene Cernan was taken December 13, 1972, by fellow astronaut Harrison Schmitt. It is in the public domain as a work created by NASA. The image has been cropped.

11. The 1919 photograph of Alvin C. York was originally copyright Underwood & Underwood. It is in the public domain because its copyright has expired.

12. The publicity photo from *The Dick Van Dyke Show* was taken circa 1963. It is in the public domain because it was published in the United States between 1923 and 1977 and without a copyright notice. Traditionally, publicity photographs are not copyrighted because of the way in which they are intended to be used.

13. The 1906 painting "Breton Church" by Emily Carr is in the public domain because its copyright has expired.

14. The photograph of First Lady Mary Todd Lincoln was taken by Mathew Brady and/or Levin Handy sometime between 1860 and 1865, and is in the public domain because its copyright has expired. It is from the Brady-Handy Photograph Collection at the Library of Congress, digital ID cwpbh.03451.

15. The 1964 publicity photo from *The Sound of Music* is in the public domain because it was published in the United States

between 1923 and 1977 and without a copyright notice. Traditionally, publicity photographs are not copyrighted because of the way in which they are intended to be used.

16. The 1951 Bowman Gum baseball card of Larry Doby is in the public domain because it was first published in the US between 1923 and 1963, and although there may or may not have been a copyright notice, the copyright was not renewed.

17. The 1923 painting "Delicate Tension" by Wassily Kandinsky is in the public domain because the artist died more than 70 years ago. It is in the collection of the Queen Sofia Museum, Madrid.

18. The 1775 painting of Samuel Johnson by Joshua Reynolds is in the public domain because its copyright has expired.

19. The 1940 publicity photo of Lupe Vélez in *The Mexican Spitfire* is in the public domain is in the public domain because it was first published in the US between 1923 and 1963, and although there may or may not have been a copyright notice, the copyright was not renewed.

20. The painting "December" by Joachim von Sandrart was created in 1642, and is in the public domain because its copyright has expired. The original can be found in the Schlossanlage Schleißheim, Germany.

21. The 2012 photograph of a large public advent calendar was taken by "Kora27" and is used here under CC BY-SA 4.0.

22. The 1912 painting "La Tasse de chocolat" by Pierre-Auguste Renoir is in the public domain because its copyright has expired.

23. The artist who created the 19th century painting of a Hanukkah celebration is unknown. The image is in the public domain because its copyright has expired.

24. The 16th century painting of St. Lucy by Benvenuto Tisi is in the public domain because its copyright has expired. The original can be found in the Capitoline Museums, Rome.

25. The photograph of a bingo card was taken by Abbey Hendrickson, and is used here under CC BY-SA 2.0. It has been cropped.

26. The photograph of Friday the 13th circled in a calendar was taken by W. J. Pilsak, and is used here under CC BY-SA 3.0.

27. The painting "December" is from the *Brevarium Grimani*, circa 1510, and is in the public domain because its copyright has expired.

28. The etching "December" by Gabriel Perrelle was created circa 1660 and is in the public domain because its copyright has expired. The image is courtesy Wellcome Images, ICV No. 7850 BR, photo V0007629EBR, and is used here under CC BY-SA 4.0.

29. The 1815 woodcut of a proposal is in the public domain because its copyright has expired.

30. The 16th century oil on lapis lazuli painting *Perseus Rescuing Andromeda* is by Giuseppe Cesari. It is in the public domain because its copyright has expired. The original object is in the collection of the Saint Louis Art Museum.

31. The 1882 painting of *Ilex aquifolium* (holly) is by Anton Hartinger, and appeared originally in the book *Atlas der Alpenflora*.

32. The 1896 drawing "December" by Eugène Grasset is in the public domain because its copyright has expired.

33. The celestial sphere is from *Scenography of the Ptolemaic Cosmography*, by Johannes van Loon, based on Andreas Cellarius's *Harmonia Macrocosmica*, 1660. It is in the public domain because its copyright has expired.

34. The 1906 automobile calendar is by Edward Penfield, and is in the collection of the Library of Congress Prints and Photographs Division. It is in the public domain because its copyright has expired.

35. The 50-year perpetual calendar photograph is in the public domain.

36. The cartoon by John T. McCutcheon is from his 1905 collection *The Mysterious Stranger and Other Cartoons by John T. McCutcheon*. It is in the public domain because its copyright has expired.

Timespinner
Press

License Description and Terms

Aside from material purely in the public domain, photographs and other material in this book are used under specific licenses permitting free use, usually with an attribution requirement. For full text and terms of these licenses, click or enter the appropriate links below. If you believe there is an error in the copyright status or attribution of any of these images, please email us.

- Creative Commons Attribution 2.0 Generic (CC-BY 2.0): http://creativecommons.org/licenses/by/2.0/deed.en
- Creative Commons Attribution-Share Alike 3.0 Generic (CC-BY-SA 3.0): http://creativecommons.org/licenses/by-sa/3.0/
- Creative Commons Attribution-Share Alike 2.5 Generic (CC-BY-SA 2.5): http://creativecommons.org/licenses/by-sa/2.5/deed.en
- Creative Commons Attribution-Share Alike 2.0 Generic (CC-BY-SA 2.0): http://creativecommons.org/licenses/by/2.0/deed.en
- Creative Commons Attribution-Share Alike 1.0 Generic (CC-BY-SA 1.0): http://creativecommons.org/licenses/by-sa/1.0/deed.en
- CC0 1.0 Universal (CC0 1.0) Public Domain Dedication (CC0 1.0) http://creativecommons.org/publicdomain/zero/1.0/deed.en
- GNU Free Documentation License (GFDL): http://en.wikipedia.org/wiki/Wikipedia:Text_of_the_GNU_Free_Documentation_License
- License Art Libre (Free Art License): http://artlibre.org

Other Books from Timespinner Press

The Story of a Special Day
Michael Dobson

A series of (eventually) 366 volumes covering everything that happened on your special day! Events, births, deaths, quotes, holidays, and much more. It's like a birthday card they'll never throw away!

US$7.95 print / US$2.99 ebook.

From Plassey to Pakistan
Humayun Mirza

The history of British Colonial India and the formation of Pakistan from the unique perspective of the son of Pakistan's first president and last of the royal line of Bengal, Bihar, and Orissa! This unique historical document tells the inside story of this distinguished family, including the detailed story of the coup that toppled his father from power!

US$27.95 print

A Whole New Navy: America's War in the Pacific

Miles Durr

The most comprehensive and detailed description of America's naval war in the Pacific ever—every battle, every ship, every task force and every task group from Pearl Harbor through the Japanese surrender! A must-have for the collection of every World War II buff!

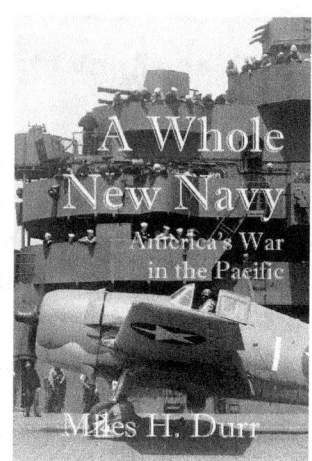

US$29.95 print

Improbable History: The Weird, the Obscure, and the Strangely Important

edited by Michael Dobson

From the birth of Western civilization to the rescue of Apollo 13, from the Leaning Tower of Pisa to Florence's Duomo, history has often turned on small, improbable details. Whatever happened to the ancient Samaritan people? Why did a fortuitous rainstorm allow the British to conquer India? How did an air raid in Italy lead to the development of chemotherapy? What happened when Albert Einstein met Adolf Hitler on the streets of Berlin? How did the Japanese manage to attack the US mainland using balloons? A cast of award-winning writers tackle some of the strangest tales in history!

US$19.95 print